Uncollected Poems

Shearsman Library Vol. 22

Books by Gustaf Sobin

POETRY

Wind Chrysalid's Rattle (Montemora, New York, 1980; 2nd edition, Shearsman Books, Bristol, 2023)
Celebration of the Sound Through (Montemora, New York, NY, 1982)
The Earth As Air (New Directions, New York, NY, 1984)
Sicilian Miniatures (Cadmus Editions, San Francisco, CA, 1986, privately distributed)
Voyaging Portraits (New Directions, New York, NY, 1988)
Breath's Burials (New Directions, New York, NY, 1995)
By the Bias of Sound: Selected Poems 1974–1994 (Talisman House, Jersey City, NJ, 1995)
Towards the Blanched Alphabets (Talisman House, Jersey City, NJ, 1998)
Articles of Light & Elation (Cadmus Editions, San Francisco, CA, 1998)
In the Name of the Neither (Talisman House, Jersey City, NJ, 2002)
The Places as Preludes (Talisman House, Jersey City, NJ, 2005)
Collected Poems (Talisman House, Greenfield, MA, 2010; 2nd edition, Shearsman Books, Bristol, 2025)
Uncollected Poems (Shearsman Books, Bristol, 2025)

FICTION

Venus Blue (Bloomsbury, London, 1991; Little, Brown, New York, NY, 1992; 2nd edition, Shearsman Books, Bristol, 2025)
Dark Mirrors (Bloomsbury, London, 1992; 2nd edition, Shearsman Books, Bristol, 2025)
The Fly-Truffler (Bloomsbury, London, 1998; Norton, New York, NY, 1999)
In Pursuit of a Vanishing Star (Norton, New York, NY, 2002)

ESSAYS

Luminous Debris: Reflecting on Vestige in Provence and Languedoc (University of California Press, Berkeley, CA, 1999)
Ladder of Shadows: Reflecting on Medieval Vestige in Provence and Languedoc (University of California Press, Berkeley, CA, 2009)
Aura: Last Essays (Counterpath Press, Denver, CO, 2009)

TRANSLATIONS

René Char: *The Brittle Age and Returning Upland* (Counterpath Press, Denver, CO, 2009)
Henri Michaux: *Ideograms in China* (New Directions, New York, NY, 2002)

Gustaf Sobin

Uncollected Poems

Edited by
Esther Sobin, Andrew Joron & Andrew Zawacki

Shearsman Books

First published in the United Kingdom in 2025 by
Shearsman Books
P.O. Box 4239
Swindon
SN3 9FN

Shearsman Books Ltd Registered Office
30–31 St. James Place, Mangotsfield, Bristol BS16 9JB
(this address not for correspondence)

EU AUTHORISED REPRESENTATIVE:
Lightning Source France
1 Av. Johannes Gutenberg, 78310 Maurepas, France
Email: compliance@lightningsource.fr

www.shearsman.com

ISBN 978-1-84861-929-6

Copyright © Gustaf Sobin, 1963, 1964, 1983, 1986, 1997
Copyright © The Estate of Gustaf Sobin, 2025
Introduction copyright © Tony Frazer, 2025

Interview with Tedi López Mills
copyright © Tedi López Mills and Gustaf Sobin, 1999,
reproduced here by kind permission of the interviewer.

The right of Gustaf Sobin to be identified as the author of this work
has been asserted by the author's Estate in accordance with the
Copyrights, Designs and Patents Act of 1988.
All rights reserved.

Contents

Acknowledgements / 7

Introduction / 8

Uncollected Poems from Magazines
(1973–2000)

Haako / 13
Pseudo-Haiku / 14
Angel / 15
Irises / 16
Il Gioco / 17
Breath Vegetal / 18
Prose 1 / 19
Where / 20
Lilacs / 21
The Poem / 22
Do Kamo / 23
On *Imagerie*: Esther Williams, 1944 / 24
O / 26
Orpheus Semantic / 27
Odes of the Extravagated / 30
Blown Bouquet / 36
Premises / 37
Like Salt, Say / 39
Where the Pine-Needles Bristle / 40
Blue, for Instance: An Essay / 42
Cosmogony / 44
Substantia / 45
Raised Stage / 46
Little Lyric for a Little Boy / 47

On the Rose Vocable of the Inviolate / 48
Father's Poem / 50

ARTICLES OF LIGHT AND ELATION / 51
(1997)

SICILIAN MINIATURES / 99
(1986)

SUSPENDED FALLS / 129

10 SHAM HAIKUS / 157
(1983)

ASCENSION / 165
(1964)

TELEGRAMS / 171
(1963)

INTERVIEW WITH TEDI LÓPEZ MILLS / 181
(1999)

Acknowledgements

The uncollected poems in the first section were first published in *Columbia Poetry Review, Denver Quarterly, Facture, Hambone, Ironwood, New Directions, Nexus, New American Writing, Nexus, Ninth Decade, Pequod, Shearsman, Sulfur, Talisman* and *Temblor*.

'Father's Poem', the author's final poem, was given to his son and has only previously appeared on Gabriel Sobin's website. It appears here with Gabriel Sobin's permission.

Articles of Light and Elation was first published in a bibliophile edition by Cadmus Editions, San Francisco, in 1997.

Sicilian Miniatures was first published in a private limited edition of 200 copies by Cadmus Editions, San Francisco, in 1986 "for friends of the poet and publisher".

Suspended Falls is a manuscript discovered in the author's papers, and appears here in print for the first time. The slight overlap with the "sham haikus" (below) suggests that it also dates from the 1980s.

Ten Sham Haikus was first published in an edition of 29 copies "in celebration of Gustaf's visit to New York City", April 1983, by The Grenfell Press, New York, 1983.

Ascension was first published in an edition of 17 copies, with an original etching, by PAB éditeur, Ribaute-les-Tavernes, Provence, in 1964.

Telegrams was first published in a private limited edition by JEA Bond, London, in 1963. A downloadable PDF edition was made available online by Duration Press in 2016.

The interview with Tedi López Mills has previously only been published in Spanish, in the interviewer's translation; it appeared in Gustaf Sobin, *Matrices de viento y de sombra* (Ediciones del Hotel Ambosmundos, Mexico City, 1999), translated by Tedi López Mills. It appears here with Tedi López Mills's permission.

INTRODUCTION

This volume of Gustaf Sobin's uncollected work offers material that *did* (mostly) see the light of day between covers, albeit, in some cases, in editions that were rather hard to find.

Given the scale of the author's official *Collected Poems* – almost 750 pages in our forthcoming new edition – it might be surprising to some readers that we have found relatively few of his poems that were uncollected. The author's papers in Yale University's Beinecke Library include a further 40 pages or so of poetry, not included here, that could be interpreted as being 'finished' poems but which were unpublished in any form. These usually exist however in multiple versions, and it is often unclear whether the author ever reached a clean final-copy stage, or whether he had just broken off, having abandoned the text. In view of this, we have decided to exclude those manuscript-only poems in favour of those that did receive the author's imprimatur and actually appeared in magazines, but were not later gathered into full collections. The relatively limited number of such uncollected poems may well be explained by the author's habit of constructing sequences from the shards and rejects of other work – see particularly the 'Caesurae', and the almost annual 'Transparent Itineraries' sequences in the *Collected Poems*. One final uncollected poem from shortly before the author's death, dedicated to his son Gabriel, was however obtained from the dedicatee, and is included here.

The two oldest publications collected here date to the period before 1973, the time when Gustaf Sobin found his poetic voice. They show glimpses of the poet's sensibility as we know it from the later work, but the 'delivery mechanism' is not yet present.

Of the two longer collections presented here, both originally issued by Cadmus Editions of San Francisco in beautiful editions, *Sicilian Miniatures* (an edition that was not released to the general public) belongs to the 'occasional' strand in Sobin's work but here spun out at greater length, in celebration of a trip to Sicily. Epiphanic poems such as these reoccur in Sobin's less public work, and *Suspended Falls* – an unpublished manuscript discovered amongst the author's papers, in which one poem overlaps with the *10 Sham Haikus* – is another. The latter was issued in a very small edition on the occasion of a visit by the author to the U.S. in 1983. Given the slight overlap, *Suspended Falls* presumably dates from roughly the same time.

Articles of Light and Elation is radically different. These poems share a likeness with the main *œuvre* in terms of their movement, but their acutely personal aspects ensure that they lie a very long way away from the more studied, modernist-inflected work where the self is often elided. Nonetheless, they deserve a larger audience than they have had hitherto, and they serve to show, perhaps, an aesthetic path deliberately not taken. It is interesting that Sobin decided to collect them as he did, given that they lie well outside the main trajectory of his work. On the other hand, I rather suspect he realised that these poems worked, and needed an audience.

Finally, this volume also includes an interview with the Mexican poet, Tedi López Mills, whose translations of Gustaf Sobin's poems appeared with the interview in a volume published in Mexico – sadly out of print at present, like the great majority of the author's work.[1] The interview has never previously been published in English.

Tony Frazer
March 2025

---

[1] Although, later in 2025, we will publish a new edition of the *Collected Poems*, and will reissue the first two novels.

Uncollected Poems

*from magazines,
plus one unpublished poem*

HAAKO

words   that wouldn't rebound   in dull
   percussions,

but being the air's potential   and reaching
into the air's uttermost muscles, as
breath   would burst, and
vibrant

shower our limbs in the light   of our spreading echo.

                    *

our words.
our echo.
but with the weight, the iridescence of other voices.

(1973)

PSEUDO-HAIKU

all night, the
scuttle of bronze over
flagstone.   at dawn, turned
forty.

(1975)

ANGEL

less, even, than naked.   lighter
faster than his wingbeats, this messenger
drawn in,
in
through his own lips; his anni-

hilated letter: gray wind . . . . shrivelled gold!

(1976)

IRISES

the *this*
that's never this.   that's lapping
tumid,

over the *that*.   doom-
heads, dream-

dancers, these
loosened scrolls that the neither,
idly,

blooms to.

(1976)

IL GIOCO

one walked
out of the other's eyes,

fed crouching
upon its own
projections: the
blood crystals it cast
upon a third.

the third
was brushing its hair,
was dreaming

of waves; wasn't
even there.

(1976)

BREATH VEGETAL

    All verbs, verbs   of unravelling.
    All light
        a darkening into ripeness; a   ripening
onto the tall   transparent stem.

                          Slipped crystals,
and the warm, wind-pitted sun. And the   lips

    suddenly limp
as the long hair spreads,
                in wet   bracelets, over   the arms.

(1976)

PROSE 1

Arose.
Against the wind in glassy wheels and the shivering of the sycamores. Stretched in their rich spindles.
To enter. Forever press. The breath forced. The skin new.
The new vowels, mumbling with roots.
With branches.
With birds gliding into their own shadows.

That enter, clamoring.

That, wider. Into the white landscapes that forever lessen.

(1976)

WHERE

      only words   could
         catch   words: keep them (our-
selves inside   them) from the flagellant whir,

      from being wingbeaten into the   else
      the ever-
             extracting   where.

                                   (1977)

LILACS

that far
for so little.   to be-
wilder yourself
in all
that hysterical lilac, the
bob and
heave, the wind
scrubbing leaf
against
leaf.   and the flowers, blinding
your fingers, that
the mouth
fill, the trough cram,
laminated,
with these living cinders.   that

far, that the
teased roots catch, the eyes
fall
through the tossed sounds of its
boughs, branches, shoots.

(1977)

THE POEM

dust caught
in those pure functions (scarcely
hindrance, but

something), the
air

rasped
against its sheer ir-
reducibles: scale-

crystals. (you'd
climbed through your eyes, and seen
them there: the words, like

in Puccio di Simone's painting,
an angel, in
a puff

of light, its peach skirts   flying
through that   hard tear).

(1978)

DO KAMO

beating
ash, or crawling, crab-

like, over
rocks . . . the

bodies
keep time, keep
light, drift

with the skull's
white shadows, their
twin

flash-
tailed fish.

this,
that: the metric in-
flexibles, the
matted, fork-
hearted
fibers.

higher, to pound
flour.   pulp
shells.   pray

to the stones
that the
stones,

budding,
be neither's.

(1978)

ON *IMAGERIE*: ESTHER WILLIAMS, 1944

only in the
milkiest
emulsions, the deepest
silvers, would
that

mirror open, the
tips

of the elbows
flare. combs, lotions . . .
her sleeves
would

float over the
foam-
white bowls with their
na-

creous blossoms. hair
shaken, hands
posed, each
glint's

a splinter, a ray I'd
pull from
those

gray, grain-
in-

flected spaces . . . .
warped
oceans, our
ob-
fuscated worlds.   would
feed on

those fires, that light
that

pours in a
limp
clatter of black,
unfastened corals . . . .

                              (1985)

O

. . . with gold, acting as
solvent, was the
    river, in fact, you'd washed; its
thin, sinuous alphabets, bleached.   lingering, now,
amongst its eddies, its mute
pools, your mouth,
your

mouth alone, our
only
riddle.

(1992)

ORPHEUS SEMANTIC

Grecque

through the mirror's
very
heart, had run
shafts, hollowed corridors.   saw you,
raw as

hair, perched
with-

in its
deepest cell. spoke, because you
couldn't. rolled you, supple
as
your own
shadows, over the
lip of

so
much stasis. these,
then, were the words, the

offerings
of the
open, the empty, of the thoroughly
ex-
tricated.

• • •

                     who, then,
in this vacuous
ballast
would save whom? through the late
drafts, driven currents, your
ankles
quiver, quick

as fish. here, where the
mouth draws

on memory alone.   where
bulky, pendulous, each organ
weighs
exactly that

of a
breath.

                     • • •

                  but no, there's
no one, nothing, you
your-

self might have echoed. but the
light as it shifts
over so much
idle decor. you, whose least glance

makes a ladder, a
scale

unto an octave in
which —heap
of whispers— the instrument itself

won't even
be

husked.   nor its
innumerable
parts,
methodically shredded.

(1993)

ODES OF THE EXTRAVAGATED

(I)

for the pages of the
voice
vanish, fast as
they' re turned. liquescent, the

very
same spaces, just
after, their glistening

residue. what
toads, or
the fat calyx of
certain marsh flowers still, some-
times,

exuded. had stopped
talking,
telling one an-
other

each other's name, the
contours, the
exact volumes our
sleep
had taken. asked yourself, occasionally,
'still there?' as your
brow

rising through the
bright

oval, came to meet
the black
liner.

        *

had let, let
one

another out, hadn't we, and
found the
im-

mensity, beyond, some-
how
smaller. was wind, though, and the un-
mistakable scent,
every-

where, of salt. of salt-
pervasive, as if
reclaiming the
very
least cavity, indentation, of

memory it-
self.   crowding it,
vacuous.

        *

'avocet,' you'd still,
oc-
casionally, as
if interject, pointing out (a relic in
it-

self) that elegant stilt, its
beak, an
up-
turned tendril.

                    (while the word itself
flew forward, a
pawn
on some illegible board, to enter al-
ready, the
al-

ready-
after).

(II)

written, the
words
become anyone's, no one's.
wouldn't need you,
now, the

flowering
fruit-

trees, what
you'd scribbled, in white
bars, across

so much
bright scoring. on that

broken
ground, its
raised chords, wouldn't even

need your-
self.

(III)

Saint Ursula, Venice

her dream, frozen in
ochre pigments, had set yours
a-
drift. so little,
now, to

keep you, the
stays, the
moorings fast to their
own
wobbling reflections. bit by
bit, had

worked free, hadn't
you? broken 'miracle' into
so
many constituent

parts. weren't
these, indeed, our

last relics, the
petal and
fracture? the pieces that still, some-
how, with-
stood?

                    swarm, then, to
what? for the
sections themselves as if
long

for deployment. your
breath, to
bud

in the very
midst
of the fresh numbers. alternately, you
are and
aren't, depending on the
sounds

you'd employ. no matter
how

fortuitous, the
kind of paradise —murmured—
you'd pro-
ject.

(1994)

BLOWN BOUQUET

about the fluffy
white hyacinths, the petals of the lilies
wrap back-
wards, splay labial. who'll keep, though,
our eyes from flying, blind
through
the

bleached calendars, glands like
bells, beating
a-

gainst neither's flanks. we, who'd
sip whispers if we could, hoard
shadows before the
light, the very
light

shattered retracted against its first
instigating
letters.

(1995)

PREMISES

as if all language were rooted in the silent grammar of an implication.

deriving from, and —inseparably— referring to.

as if, indeed, there were two languages: our own, which is perfectly audible, articulate, appreciable, and another —uninterruptedly mute— which is never more than the taut, vibratory surface of the implicated.

but the *frappe* of so much white letter.

what our own words aspire, reach towards, as if to imbue themselves with the sonorous luster of their own origins.

. . . in, say, a sheer coincidence of mass . . .

what we can only qualify (bound as we are to analogy, metaphor, conceit) as their confiscated mirror.

as, in sort, an etymology abandoned in the exact same instant as its formulation.

for words by their very nature, fall into the shadow of their faceted parts; by their very agreements, undergo eclipse.

the breath catching on its own viscosity.

sublunar, subliminal, nothing's written, in effect, that's not under-written: no world, in effect, that's not —ultimately— underworld.

within which —dense nexus— alluded.

having gutted the heart of every humor but its strange, abstract effulgence: its counter-trope.

whereby, on certain days, certain creatures, beautiful in the bulk of their luminous particles: in so much pure, undifferentiated mass.

whereby less, even lesser, as it flexes with magnitude.

stripped, finally, of all gods, scriptures, all myth but the living mineral of the eyes as they vanish, now, beneath the roll of their own lashes.

whereby the word: the word-wordless: what would enter, now, the sheer immediacy of the remote.

wedging, as it did, that vaporous expanse: what had been, until then, meticulously withheld.

. . . the null, at last, as if invested . . .

in the rhyme of those matched annunciates rendered palpable.

. . . there, just there, where the
mouth rounds to
its
scuttled rose, even the silence,
suddenly, would have
grown

re-
verberant.

(1995)

LIKE SALT, SAY

neither the word nor its
echo, not even
the

slake-marks that an echo
might have left
on

the scorched surface of
some
murmur, like

salt, say,
still glowing in its
reliquary when all else,

decidedly, had
long since
dis-

sipated.

(1996)

WHERE THE PINE-NEEDLES BRISTLE

where the pine-
needles bristle, like
blue
sequins, the

mirrors
burn.   so

many knuckles
for that
hand-

ful of
words: path
springing—mineral—
out

of path.   wind I
drop
through, sleep
in, a lobe wrapt
in

the plump
muscles of a mouth . . .

*

knead and
grapple.   bury us in
that

breathing.   for
earth's

its own
twin.   that
pressed, the

bodies im-
print.   print canyons,
thistles.   rise,
wet-

flanked,
from the driven image
of our

own ir-
retrievable
limbs.

(1997)

BLUE, FOR INSTANCE: AN ESSAY

. . . done nothing more, finally, than
measure interval,
the
sporadic fractures in the very midst of the
air's otherwise
con-

solidated structure. was what, occasionally,
you'd glimpsed: blue, for
instance,
be-

tween the now-all-but-perfected flow of the
ir-
remediable. yes, wet, be-
wildering, the stray particles, you'd
called them, of that
once

substantiating grammar. would dwell, wouldn't
you, in each of those
al-
ready vanishing interludes: lay wrapt, say, be-

neath the coils of so many
blind,
adamant lashes. with wind, here, on
one side, rocks on another, the
breath moves, residual,
be-

tween. what holds, holds to nothing, really, but shattered
sequence. was why murmur
would round
to
orifice. would press, insistent. yes, was why,
mesmerized, you'd
draw, if you could, at the

very tissues of your
own al-

ready dis-
solving message.

(1997)

COSMOGONY

having sipped the
   mirror to a single, ir-
reflexive bead, a
no-

breath, saw the cold, slow-
burning cell-stars
bunch in
con-

junction.

(1997)

SUBSTANTIA

. . . were nothing more, you knew, than the
recipient of
that grey, prismatic gaze, reflection in which, having
hardened to
a

form, felt yourself shatter, faceted, into
so
many sonorous parts.

(1997)

RAISED STAGE

. . . their mirrors aflame, they're
licking at
smoke, at the thin
hissing sparks —stigmatic rays— they've

generated. who, whose, this wedged
decor, this spectacle
with-

out spectators if not the
nobody's, bodies locked syncretic to the
labor of their own
un-

making. fume, that billowing
flower, the throw of
its

somnolent ash. see them, now, as they
sip, drawing, now, on nothing; no,
nothing what-
so-

ever, while their lashes clamp shut a-
gainst their own
in-

eluctable dis-
solving.

(2000)

LITTLE LYRIC FOR A LITTLE BOY

. . . just as pear trees come up cream and
almonds
ice, the heart, in a spray of imperceptibles,

wreathes itself in air, in a
whirring disk of
self-

astonishments.   weightless, the heart's
weightless, little
Neil, and knows itself only in

echo, in
those notes
pitched fortuitous towards another's

consummate ac-
cording.   peer, then, into flower, flame; draw
feature from the

dragonfly and
thunder-
bolt, from the gaze that wraps you, this very

instant, in the tissues of something far
more weightless
yet.

(2000)

ON THE ROSE VOCABLE OF THE INVIOLATE

frivolous with immensity, let your
fingertips slip over the
very contours of
inception, grazing as they did its pleats, ripples, the

slick
contracted expanse of its muscles, laminated
in

dark oils. loom and
dissolve; heave and succumb. for here, furtive, epi-

phenomenal, you'd only transit —nebulous— through all
those flexed
de-
terminants. does the
mirror know what the mirrored doesn't? had the

echo entered, rooted resplendent, there where the
voice
manifestly couldn't? for here, even the air's

for burial. and so, too, each
tended member, its least
emitted murmur,
the

poem itself as precedent, but only wrapped, enclosed in the
whirring viscera of its own
word-
less origins. oh ocean in the

rose vocable of the in-
violate, let
breath be crossed with
blood, and
blood rotate in the empty orbits of its own all-
                              enveloping aureole.

                                                            (2000)

FATHER'S POEM

for Gabriel

. . . too late to do anything, now, but
begin. but recycle the spent stars on their
dec-
imated orbits— and dahlias too. yes, dahlias, and
the blown tulips, flaked well beyond the bleached
frescoes of
memory. carve, then, for certainly the translucent
                                                           pores of the
fingers will swell to what the hands, in all their
rapacity, had long since
obliterated.

                                                               (2005)

Articles of Light and Elation

    endlessly, you write the tips of
my fingers. mistake me
       for the dark signs, that dark light you conceal
   in the bunched coil of your loins. draw figs, draw
         flowers, while the wind stiffens
              with the steady drafting of these rhymes.

    blonde, already, with light, my
mouth fills with that sudden resin.   moon and
       cypress, and through your thin, breath-
    quickened shanks, these hills, in the spray of
                   their thistles, solidly driven.

    no greater nudity than your tears, were what
I'd sipped into
        thin pellets of sound: madrigals of wind and
    shadow, and these late daisies, worked
                azurous, about the
                        narrow whorl of your ears.

    by avoiding your own
burnished mirrors, made
        chords, formed unions out of each,
       occulted section, the very measures I'd
              rise to, and move in: pleat into these, your
                                portrait's first
                                      delineations.

because, ever since, even the rocks
have lain open. violet, agape, won't close
    without that sheath of signs, hiss
of whispers that your
              breath, in half-breaths,
                        blows adamant into mine.

    so much torque for
hurtling four, whistling turbines into a distance, thin
      as the crisp linens you'd
  twist to, ankles
           arched flat and fingers, in
                    that furious arabesque, forked.

far below, three clouds, narrow as
needlefish, drift downwind.   'now,' I say to
    nothing but the altitude that lessens, and
  this image —its wrapped mirrors— I bring you that, touched,
                      shall simultaneously
                                    glisten.

what brought me to the very edge, and made
even your earrings —yes, these— the very emblems
      of air; on the far side
    of our mirror's black backing, their un-
                            suckled pearls, fulgurous.

    under a pale rain of ginkgo leaves, their brass fans
spread flat, had pulled
        at your roots, your
    hair wired wild to my fists.   were words.   were
            teeth, too, and the piled weight of
                        our lives, what we steadily
                              pummelled weightless.

over the puffed white sleeves
of your blouse, your endless eyes
      stare backwards, buoying me in
this elision of sound. what words, though, would
           keep your image from drowning, pale sapphire,
                in all that outrage of bronze?

    together, lay like
two pages pressed within a
        botany of seething, wind-scuttled shadows. each,
   each other's memory, cupped the
           bulk of our organs, dense, against our
                very dismembering, earth's otherwise
                        omnivorous dark.

there where the goad
drove your gold hair over, entered the
    moving frieze of so
    many mirrored adjustments.   slick with
                myth, loved it —just there—
                      where I'd vanish; where you, rising,
                          only accrued.

would bring it, at long last, to an end, this
distance, this 'self' as separate.   dense,
   dense with unknowing, would ram absence
  with its own petals, bring my
       full weight wet, impacted,
           against its vaporous contours, that chimeric
                                                mask.

  the lit candle's
your color. everywhere, you
    carry candles, their plump, vertiginous buds. even
   here, where you aren't, my
      room's lit with the ring of your hands, and
         this, this: the
           flushed heart that it ravishes.

> we only meet, now, in letters, language, in
> those locked granaries of
>   perpetual deferment.   what if, one
>   day, it were to end, begin, the verb burst, and
>   our bodies, shivering, break from
>   their pods: wind-straight, steel-hard.

   wrote, usually, for your
ears, their heavily
      petalled lobes. this, though, is for your
   mouth, that my silence
              might enter yours, might fill you mute
                    with so much rung,
                            redundant tissue.

   you, more *fauna* than
flora, have carved my very mirrors, brought
     my dark eyes level with your
   soft, odiferous horns.   what if the
         arrow were to enter, shattering, as it
             did, into a plethora of
                fat, evanescent pearls?

with each thrust wider, more
winged, that exquisite
      construction (what worked, now, to an
  amber, holds us captive in its glowing
              dome, enveloped already in all
                          that vaulted
                                  liquescence).

  only entered, finally, do you finally
enter, your
    cave crammed luminous with its own flowers, and
 that slap, that flapping, that insistence
     that pins each petal to a far deeper
          efflorescence.

    only overwhelmed, only
then, only *that*, finally, that
        matters (the whole floor
            gone buoyant, afloat on our own
                releases, as your long eyes, lidded,
                          squint venetian).

    the loops fill, fill
tumescent; you carry them —their tumescence— like
      two, identical trophies.   in your tall mirrors, now, a
    full ocean away, you
            toy with their fires; draw, as
                        from straws, their glitter liquescent.

  …with those other brushes (the
minuscule) you'd attended
    to your own portrait, preparing, in
  tiny touches, that oval, that image unimaginable, that
      effigy I bear embedded that, striking
        its tall mirrors, had ricocheted gold.

    the 'thrust of life,' you
taught me, is towards its own
        astonished tissues, the heart
    plucked rose out of the
                cold shrubbery of so much commotion; a
                          nest ablaze in the breath's
                                  abeyance.

    deaf, now, in the narrow

clutch of your thighs, pulled the lily —the lily-

        successive— free

of its wet fires.   a-

            drift, now, on this floating altar, oh so

                      many shaken petals for spelling a

                                single, unbroken name.

closer, now, to Tiepolo's nacres, his
skies extravagant, to that breath
      barely embodied, being so light, so lit, so eminently
lifted, rose buoyant through your words, yesterday, into
          this, this: this elsewhere
                    that otherwise isn't.

   my lips, taking the
fine line of your brows, the gorgeous domes of
    your still-
  dreaming lids, traced flame to its
      crowded flowers. just there, from its
           soundlessness, sipped.

    like water birds, breaking the
mirror for the
       live morsels beneath, pulled quivers, our deep, still-
  shivering skeins, one
            from another.   later, lay as if
                drifting, linens taut
                      over so much disrupted depth.

    there where the marble's piled, driven
deep into the ephemera of its own
        reflections, we —finally— come free,
   quit sequence, happen
                upon this poem that pulls us, sinuous,
                          into its dark, involuted drafts.

    blonde through black, saw your long hair
slip funneled. often, though, wore
        nothing; wore what my palms pulled taut
over your raised buttocks, and the waters aped, wild
          with so much slapped marble, steadily
                  distended piling.

  watched you in all your
wild, unraked blondness ('cable,' I'd
    called it) working – teeth and fingers – at so
many multi-podded succulents. was it the moon
      that made life so lavish, these days, or
        this, its watery gold mirrors into
          which, readily, it vanished.

as with the fresh water, here, lying dormant
beneath the salt, had
    begun tapping our own lives for
yet another, for those ob-
        fuscated depths wherein, already,
            we'd draw image, sip —turgid— our
                  wrested shapes.

    there, where the deep bells
beat air, we, too, might have risen, entered, at
       long last, that very instant that eradicates
        all others.   might have found ourselves dressed in
           the weightless fabric of our gazes,
              that blue gauze
                  salvaged from such suddenly evacuated spaces.

(Ca' d'Oro)

    not the one that your hand draws, but
that your head shakes
        into such a wheel of washed fire I'm
    left dazzled in the late light of a world I'd
            thought vanished. I rub your temples with
                my palms, hold you against my own dark, glowing.

 crossing Lombardy, you in a
breathing sheath of
  blue polka dots, whispered to one an-
 other our singular fate, the *basso*
    continuo of some yet
      inaudible work, underpinning of its airs,
      evanescent variations.

    now that I've taken you (who aren't
even here) into that high room with its
        hard sheets, wisteria
      sashed to the rafters overhead, would bury myself in
          that wild cable.   haul you under, and
                bury us both in that sudden bewildering,
                         diadem ablaze
                                beneath shut lids.

    here, in the already
flowering hills, still
        heard barges, the early morning's
        washed haulage (there, where
            every ray of your hair had held me in the
                slow lash of its writhing, its
                      tentacular retractions).

    you, at last, smelling exactly
like your letters, envelopes, would burst
        from a whole ocean's abstract into so
    many adored particulars.   would emerge, from your very
           own phrases, shimmering. oh no nudity's that
                of our breaths'
                      first knot.

                              (*physical mysteries, one*)
    cradled incipient within the
flooded sack, your
        each feature *in potentia*.   oh toys, figs for
    your fingertips, what expelled
                    would coat you, diaphanous, in its
                            shimmering membrane; wrap you, in its
                                    slick films, transfigurant.

                              (physical mysteries, two)
     carried you, thus – your image – within my
 matched glands imminent.   even here, higher, where the
         irises rise rammed into the sun's
     showering freckles, brought you (who weren't
                 even here) turgid towards your each
                     distinct feature. these fluids, thus,
                             await only their fires.

(physical mysteries, three)

   what leaps liquescent
leaps from the deepest mirrors, the
      most cherished deposits.   is yours, your image-
   iconic, that you've wrested free; through your
          rung mouth cajoled.   oh so many opals
             running flushed, now, over
                    fingers, forehead, teeth.

                              (*physical mysteries, four*)
...shook the very
last drops of that mirror free, then ran them, an
    unctuous membrane, over your flushed
    and now glowing visage.   oh miracle
              of so much effigy pressed, pummelled, its
                    tissues those
                          of a goldbeater's sheath.

                              (*nightingales*)
the deeper the thicket, the more liquid, sustained the
vibrato.   clandestine, too, their lyric
     muscles us in its
  foliage, urges us through its measures for-
            ward.   stills our whispers, finally, like
                   so much distant, still-
                            incandescent lightning.

    there, within the wheat's
darkest heart, would thresh
        one another rose.   would bring you, twice blonde, to
    those successive
             effusions.   under the piled
                 winds, sip you to the very twinge, very
                       throb, very rupture of each wild,
                             syncretic germination.

    there where your curls
moved down over mine, my thighs
        went blind, went
           blonde with your writhing.   each
                time urged, othered, mythed to
                      that immensity, the warp goes sleek
                            with so much unabated lathing.

    you'd worked, molded
me weightless.   unto
       no one, nothing finally, you'd
   brought me unto these spaces that *aren't*.   oh ebullience
          of being nothing, your breath thoroughly rounded
                 about so much white.

    for 'life' in itself isn't alive, only
that —those— who
        receive and bestow it, the dark
    daisy chains of gesture and movement, thrust
           and recoil; of you, this very instant rising, my glitter
                within you, and this, this, that we'd
                      never heard, yet find ourselves uttering.

Sicilian Miniatures

(Palermo)

as the boat's
motors cut, like a
hood the
heat falls.

like pans, beaten
fast, rhythmic
sputter
of a black tugboat

high crumbling façades,
facing south, small
bars
beneath

down, through the
narrow streets, aired them-
selves
on damp shadow.

short men seated
under straw
hats, trays of
iced squid, floating past.

always a chair
at every door; someone
watching
who won't see.

matters: how quick the
eyes
move, which way
the back's faced . . .

low moon, long
sea — across
so much
space, carried sedatives.

like some slippery, ice-
cold fish
swallowed alive: *acqua
gassosa*.

grapes, like
majolica, the very
image
of grapes . . .

through a spray
of gray beads, the scent
of oils,
unguents . . .

(Sicilian fan)

as its spines
spread open: hazy
violets, and a distant
pastorale.

even in mid-
summer, small fires, smoke
through
magnolias.

(street shrine 1)

a Mary, swooning
doll-
like, in an oval
of white lightbulbs.

(street shrine 2)

an aureole of
neon
catching — magenta —
upon the gaudy thorns.

of myself, no
word, no
messages; would wake early, take
trains to the temples.

stout stations in the
midst of
nowhere: black
waiting rooms, within.

through the
high, rolling
interior: raised earth,
cradled air.

dry wind, dry
rocks, not
even the beggars, there,
say thanks.

light, like an
hallucinogen (black, the
back halves
of the lemons).

(Segesta)

way that the ruins
gape, won't
close, that the tourists
keep turning.

high, over the last
half-
circles, *contadini*
setting the grasses afire.

thrashed branches; almonds,
falling husked,
into fish-
nets.

over the seared
hills, their rolling
black
rectangles: the sea.

flat-
roofed. already
Africa: Tràpani, where the boats leave
for the islands.

slips dark, past the
rose-
incrusted stuccos, the pilot's
launch.

thick cables
of brown hair, quick
fingers
picking at squid.

domes, blown glass-
like, mammiferous, over the
low
smoking sheds . . .

sprinkled myself, all
night, with ice-
water: *scirocco*, the
white-eyed!

of them, of
theirs — errant, too, and carrying
nothing ex-
cept the letter.

(Agrigento)

waited at a long
low-awninged café for the
late
light at the temples.

a moon moving
over the un-
capped
columns: lost digit.

stone drums, stacked
into rows of
brown
tubulous lilies.

(vase)

out of the earliest
geometries, it's the animals
that evolve: animals,
fish, gods . . .

(vase: night scene)

their bracelets, even
the fronds a-
bout them — like
octopi — *alight!*

(koré)

falls, like
waves, foam-cloth, from the
raised breast, the
fresh rhythms.

through glass. not
Nike but the
Sphinx, my cast
reflections, travelling across.

(Siracusa)

lovely walking to the
very end of
things: port fortresses, fine
spray.

coins, like
tiny
paperweights, on the fluttering
green chits.

face, half-wrapped in
hair, glances
fast
as a needle-fish.

(Catania)

curtains, in blown
folds, deep
through a
dark butcher's.

tin sheds and
palazzi; a toothpick, tongue-
rolled, over
an unwavering lip.

utterly relinquished, un-
earthed, tremolo of a
nun at
vespers.

below the
rose domes, green
as leaves, the
young oranges . . .

heat falling in
white circles,
wells
of the catacombs.

one, meticulous,
black-
beaded stickpin holds
the whole veil on.

with skinny rolls of
coins, nuns
buying bus tickets
for Caltanissetta.

travelling back, now, note-
books soft
with sweat, palaces flickering
saffron, then blue.

oleanders flying past, the
headcloths flap
like bright
little blindfolds.

just off the
white
excavations, a tanker
taking the roll . . .

(fishmonger)

sprinkles his
wooden cases, keeps
the pink
squid writhing.

slabs of chopped
ray, an
eye — sometimes — in the midst
of the meat.

really two
worlds, this light, that
dark, these fingers
swimming through . . .

(tramp steamer, dusk)

over its row of
wet
wavering candles, moors
diaphanous.

no word, no
messages.   but limp, and ribbed
in moonlight, my scattered
clothes.

. . . rotting
fruit, stacked
rubble.   only from the sea, once again,
saw domes.

Suspended Falls

*(An Essay on the Cadence of Disclosure
Illustrated by Fifty-two Four-line Poems)*

a moon, as it
rises, over the moon-
white
boulders.

lights
of the hill villages:
phosphorescent
tattoos.

too high, shrill
to be dogs, the
lunar
foxes.

(*a Van Gogh armchair*)

straw, like
blond
viscera, burst
from under.

fat, the
shafts
of white iris in
water.

what
with the first warmth, a woman
—quick with
ribbons— trellising shoots.

lets go
of its little ghosts, the
wind-
snapped linen.

even in this
unending mistral, the
blossoms
keep coming.

where poppies, to the very
tips of
the blue grain,
bob.

as crows, in a
wave, swing
free of
the cherries.

a week
working the irises,
a single night,
no moon.

(*the web*)

dew outlines
the entire diamond,
even
its rays.

where,through the bluest
of greens,
goldfish
drift.

(cyclists 1)

hair
swept flat, shirt vibrating
like a wind-
struck awning.

(cyclists 2)

through the long
curves, downhill, cyclists
'just
like snakes.'

cherries low, now
over the
breeze-
headed poppies.

like an army of
javelins, cane
angled
jade.

(*wind-tramp*)

collapses, in a
heap of
sound.   of *bornes*, kilometer-
stones, oblivious.

like
little bones, snapping, a
cloud of
jackdaws, at dawn.

a shadow flat
across barley, up
over
cypress, Sunday's biplane.

(cucumbers)

as steel
slips —visible— beneath the
icy
white slices.

'as if
floating on water,' poppies in a
wide,
windy field.

throbs, like
jellyfish, the
night's
blue lightning.

like a
lung —now— the wind fills,
empties the room
of jasmine.

rained so hard
rained even
in Esther's
dreams . . . .

off the tall
rafters, now, the sun in
long,
burning drops.

long whir, short
tap of
those blue-
skirted crickets.

(*boules*)

with three,
four puffs of dust, the
spheres
come to a stop.

(*Sorgue 1*)

on itself the
Sorgue
floats, lacquering
its long, red-headed weeds.

(*Sorgue 2*)

. . . jade that the
trout
speckles, that its
muscle whips, unrippling.

. . . sizzle, like
crossed wires, the
glass-
eyed *cigales*.

flies, ringing the
ankles, as the
thunder
grows.

rises over and
over a-
gainst a ceiling that beats
it back.

(*Les Marocaines*)

at the waterfalls, Sunday,
their
des-
olate perfumes.

like reliquary knuckles,
knobs of the
dead
anemones.

as a magpie
stabs —sideways— at a
black
almond.

from that bitter,
breath-
wrinkled wine, sipped
midges.

(*grapes*)

thud, like heart-
beats, into the hollow
black
buckets.

on the base
of a broken jar, that
broken
syllable: *ix.*

from Gabelli's burst
red
firecrackers, the faded
pink petals.

down, through the
first
cold raindrops, a hornet
hung gold.

. . . air
shimmying where a
peasant forks
fire.

in the long
rain, the new wine's
even
greener.

through mist, white
cypresses and the
huge
moon of the sun . . . .

woodsmoke, ragged,
over the
ice-
white roof tiles.

. . . instant the
rain
stopped tickling on the
roof tiles —snow.

gray blades of the
lavender, what the
snow
duplicated white . . . .

the moon, chipped
blue; icicles
like
Chinese beards . . . .

(borie en demi-lune)

lunar, the
stone hovel, its
snow-
pitted half, facing north.

sight visored to a
vine row, was so
cold the
finch flew toward us . . . .

the snow, finally, as
it vanishes; the wheat, sheets
of
emerald.

. . . lighting the
glass kerosene lantern,
a face as it
fills.

10 Sham Haikus

for my friend, Bradford Morrow

a week
working the irises;
a single night,
the moon.

lights
of the hill villages:
phosphorescent
tattoos.

too high, shrill,
to be dogs, the
lunar
foxes.

lets go
of its little ghosts, the
wind-
snapped linen.

(l'aube au ballet russe)
black rose, and a
silver
stickpin moon.

even in this
unending mistral, the
blossoms
keep coming.

cherries low
over the
breeze-
headed poppies.

at dusk, a
hand-
ful of fire.

from that bitter,
breath-
wrinkled wine, sipped
midges.

. . . . lighting the
glass kerosene lantern,
a face as it
fills.

Ascension

I ascend from inseparable noon:

I, the elongation of me: myself

Pebble-eyed, peripheral, aligned
By the sun. Axle-spun I assume
   my new symmetry: a colossus

Green-limbed among the orchards
Liberating apples. I extend; I

Advance (an earth, refuting the
 cage of its ribs) retrieving,

Twin-spoked, my equivocal self.

Telegrams

To R.C.

The poet: a metaphysician whose only chore is in the description of circles.

*

The poet: the pontifex, the builder of bridges. Depart from a known point, a material position. Light upon the mystical: the realm of the poet. Relate one to the other through an elliptic return.

*

The muses don't descend: they're omnipresent.

*

Obsession with the poetic process: an obsession no less relevant than, in other days, with magic, alchemy, divine revelation or the deciphering of a thunderbolt.

*

To begin anew: my notebooks filled with the anxiety of blank pages; my fingers, with the excitement of sea departures.

*

Awareness, not intellect: that is my concern; and to open the doors onto the star gardens of wonder: that is my relevance.

*

In the great ellipse that arcs our presence, I shall be the alchemist: my words shall be the precious metal of our dust: I shall catch you like a sand crab with a scavenger's phrase. You shall be, my love, not portrayed but existent; your golden knees shall move beneath the sheets of my pages.

*

The poet's alchemy: to translate emotion into reason, and reason into syllabic action.

*

Contact assured with a passing cod troller (festooned with nets) by means of the heliograph. I marvel at this communication: man speaking with the voice of the sun.

*

To relocate oneself resetting the wrist upon the arm, the word upon the tongue. To reassemble: the moon trysting with the mollusk.

*

The meteor: the poem. Conceived in primal flames and destined, by its own lucidity, toward the destruction of all but essence, traverses a quadrant no wider than the hips of the pomegranate. Praise to the meteor, the white message, and to the goddess of the Perseids.

*

I'm with you already, my love. We exist beneath the same wind, the same wheeling birds. The anchors in the roadstead have secured our equanimity.

*

I spin upon the equator of an elm tree axis with memory a root and promise a node of green ascendancy.

*

Each morning the poet, like the astronomer, must collect the powder of meteors from his rooftops.

*

Because your fingers are golden fronds, yielding me the produce of a breakfast serenity: almonds of prayer and lemons of innocence, I am more than myself. I am the morning sun, weaned upon the fruits of my solstice.

*

You shouldn't be surprised, in our conversations, if I speak my poems. I seek a commonplace mystique.

*

The woman shall inform you of the flower's specie. You, in turn, shall tell her of its meaning.

*

Between ignorance and knowledge: enlightenment. Between knowledge and revelation: poetry.

*

A kinship with Fra Angelico. Your frescoes lie still wet upon the friar's cell: their edge extending onto the ceiling, onto the sky. You bend the angel's wing. You prepare his ascension.

*

The wind, through the shutter doors, delivered me a green leaf: a gift, lying among my stale papers. I shall seek, forever, a fitting retribution.

*

You are my brother by bloodstream and more so by correlation: I watch the masonry of your design blooming each morning into an arbor, an arch: built to the measure of man's shoulders. I watch without discerning the stone from the shrub and the underpinnings of a scrambling lizard.

*

Man's preoccupation with magic numbers: Pythagorean music, Christian adoration of the Trinity, Cartesian mathematics. I abide by the mystery of one. My symbol: the infinite. My obsession: their inseparability.

*

The poem is a shard, produced from the soil: a fraction of a buried numeral.

*

I come across the plain, the wind within my satchel, the words in quest upon my fingernails, needing a druggist, an alchemist to translate the cryptic branches of my bones. I come seeking myself in calcium fruition.

*

Kinship of the poet and the peasant: both, intermediaries in capricious fruit.

*

The compass shall not forget your direction nor the sundial your shadow. Your work shall be a perpetual solace to the vagrant: the people of the valley. They shall delight forever in the veracity of your knuckles.

*

Progress is, in fact, regression: a return to the innocence of one's first orange and the wonder of its difference from the sun.

*

I seek a chapel less deserted than the last. Instead, I'm greeted by a billy goat, laughing from a belfry.

*

His presence in the village caused a great stir. The populace (gathered in the shade of their ramparts, picking herbs) wondered if he wasn't the holder of the mysterious deeds, or perhaps, the forerunner of another onslaught. He, on his part, was equally bewildered. He had forgotten the relevance of his own footfalls.

*

A poem: an aviary without cages.

*

Iron man shall be forged by the hammer of the sky upon the anvil of the earth. His incorruptible presence shall bear the marks of his blacksmith.

*

The poem assembles the past with the present; affirms the present with its impossible future.

*

Bury your hopes in the shade of an umbrella pine: they shall sprout into a green celebration of fulfilment.

*

My bamboo walking stick (a standard of the jungles) sets in motion the motion of my steps, the metronome of my blood. It regulates my turgid pleasures, stark beneath the camphors. My walking stick: it has a mace-head of stars and a stub of crickets.

*

Hidden among the reeds are the gods (like women without blemish, like plums without winter); concealed along the pathway of the poet, raising his scythe.

*

The color of the earth is upon my skin; the wind, upon my breath. I shall not scrape, from my fingernails, the stars.

*

After four days on the plateau, I return. My satchel is filled with rocks, a puma's skull and some mint leaves pressed in a notebook of new poems. I treat each with an equal delight.

*

To return to the wood table, stark with promise, to the lead stub and the stars for companionship. To indulge oneself in celibacy.

*

The sun is my clock. The owl my nocturnal accomplice.

*

Your tresses are bound in a lofty triumph: let a goldfinch prepare them for your pillows.

*

As soon as the amphora assumes the shape of its bearer, the stars shall lie harmoniously in the soul's ephemeris.

*

Our work is done for the day. Our pencils lie in the toolshed; our papers, among the secrets of the flowering pear. We find solace tonight: two brothers in the commerce of words and bread. We share the lamb. We heed the woman: she brings to our table the wine of our sustenance. Together, we form a single triptych. Our incense burns on the hearth; our candles, a wish of smoke upon the chimney pots.

Interview with
Tedi López Mills

My first questions are necessarily biographical.

What made you leave the United States in the first place and what took you to France?

France was refuge. I grew up in Cold War America, dominated throughout the 1950s by an ultra-conservative Cold War aesthetics. For me, the model of the artist already lay elsewhere both in time and space. It was deeply associated with that of the 1920s expatriate living abroad and practicing/propagating the ideals of a certain modernism: "Make it new," etc. From that movement, I came to see and, eventually, explore the possibilities of an art that generated, rather than simply replicated, a vision of existence: a language that had the power to qualify – re-qualify – the very materials it was normally called upon merely to convey. It was drawn, that is, far more by the means, the conduits, the vehicles of language than the need to express myself, say, in some particular manner about some particular subject with some particular voice. Then as now, the mysteries lay far more in the conveyor than the conveyed.

In terms of reading, I can trace my itinerary virtually step by step. It began, at age fifteen, with the novels of Ernest Hemingway. I felt drawn already by the image of the artist-in-exile questioning the values of his own generation from a certain privileged distance. It was an image that helped me break from the rigid provincialism of my own generation. It offered alternatives.

More than merely reading Hemingway, I had the good fortune of meeting him a number of times throughout the 1950s at his *finca* near Havana. Totally unlike the public, publicized image, Hemingway struck me as one of the gentlest, even shyest individuals I've ever met, full of consideration for his guests, full of intense listening. Reading Hemingway would lead, soon enough, to Pound, and Pound, in one direction, to the troubadours (yes, Provence already), and, in another, to Eliot, Eliot's translation of St. John Perse's *Anabase*, and from there, onto modern French poetry in general. My literary itinerary had already been traced, it would seem, from the very start. But much of it, I'd like to think, began in Havana in the early 1950s: outside, that is, the *diktats* of Anglo-American conservatism and already immersed, to a certain extent, in a *culture cosmopolite*.

Why did you stay in France and why did you choose this particular geography: Provence, that is?

Ideally, one chooses a place, a landscape, a particular geography for all its inherent resemblances. Within its rocks, winds, clouds, one comes to recognize the otherwise undisclosed parts of one's inner being: one's own, yet-to-be-articulated vision. So it was with Provence. It offered, from the very start, a fully coherent set of material counterparts for everything that still lay undeclared – impalpable – within. It offered, in short, a mirror for reflecting upon my own invisibilities. Fluid, moving, an astonishing composite of wilderness and rich, intensely cultivated fields, lying subject – twelve months a year – to a regime of thirty-two distinct winds, Provence, for me, was already a book: a book that begged to be written.

Beyond those natural attributes, lay, of course, the cultural. For it's a land that basks in the very light that once gave birth to Western civilization. Mediterranean by nature, Provence is not only a place of grapes and olives but one redolent with measure, proportion, with that antique division of space into sacred and profane. Even today, it seems charged with the memory of that earliest humanism. Here, one can not only wander through a pure, Virgilian landscape, one can breathe – occasionally – its very air. Assimilate its still seething particles. Was I, in my own personal search, travelling backwards? Reaching, in a crepuscular age, towards the vestiges, at least, of that inaugural moment? I suspect so.

Lastly, I'd add to the many attributes of this land its silences, its voids. It not only "speaks," it omits, creates lacunae, whole areas of what might be called "the non-denominated." Despite its great antiquity, it's a land, I feel, that hasn't yet been done, depleted, verbally exhausted. To the contrary, it generates – thanks to those blank expanses – the empty pages of so much empty, ongoing space. Therein, everything – it would seem – might *still* be said.

Could you describe the voyage, literary and otherwise, that brought you to Provence?

I see someone arriving at the Gare d'Avignon in the icy cold winter of 1963 with nothing more than a single bag, a briefcase, and a somewhat exalted – if perfectly vague – intuition. I've always operated, in fact, out of intuition, out of the tenuous threads of so many instinctive, unsolicited signals. It's this that's always guided me, indicated – in a kind of pre-linguistic grammar of its own – the direction I needed to take. As for the intellect, I've never considered it as anything more than an agent in the service of that intuition. For it's the intuition, as I see it, that informs, and the intellect, in pursuit, that comes to substantiate.

So there I was with my bag, briefcase and intuition: with, that is, a certain premonition of what lay ahead but without the slightest idea of how to attain it. For how does one begin to express in words what needs to remain – by its very essence-wordless? To circumscribe, in sorts, an omission? It would take ten full years of failure, self-doubt and intense migraine before I'd come to write the first, hesitant lines of a verse I could call my own: to translate into poetry what was, after all, little more than the beating of butterfly wings against the cage of the psyche. Ten years in which to fashion, that is, a syntax open – empty – enough to include those very omissions.

Tell me about René Char. How did you discover his work and what was your friendship with him like?

René Char's influence was determinant in terms of both my life and work. I came across his poetry while still living in the United States. From the very first page, I remember, I felt enthralled, illuminated. There was a level of urgency, necessity in his verse such as I'd never seen elsewhere, a seriousness in regard to the art of poetry that struck me as utterly devotional. It's from Char that I'd come to consider poetry as recourse: an elevated level of rhetoric in which all the disparate elements of one's experience might not only find their place but discover, therein, the very octaves of their unravelling.

Char himself was abundantly kind, generous, protective, inspirational. For me, he was every bit as much a "father figure" in the affective sense as he was *maître*: the craftsman of an art in which I more than gratefully accepted the role of apprentice. He was, however, often disproportionate in his judgments. In my own case, I know, he had an exaggerated sense of my own capacities as a poet, even during those ten years when I produced perfectly nothing. I've often felt that I've done little more in my creative life than attempt to match René Char's high expectations, be equal – that is – to all his affectionate hyperbole.

Where would you place your poetry in the American and French canons? What tradition would you link yourself with, what "anxiety of influences"?

I feel every bit as close to the prosody of Gerard Manley Hopkins as I do to the visionary aesthetics of Mallarmé. Given the diversity of influences at play in my work (in *any* poet's work, today), I couldn't begin to situate my verse in relation to any established canon. Furthermore, one always ventures, explores, doesn't one, in defiance of canon. This being said, I feel my own work can be associated, if anywhere, with a certain tradition in American poetry that begins with William Carlos Williams, continues with the Objectivists, most especially George Oppen, and runs, today, throughout the work of Creeley, Snyder, McClure. Within that tradition, one finds a poetry profoundly involved with its age, scrupulously mindful of particulars, discreet if not downright self-effacing in regard to the personal self, and charged with an innate faith in the power of language as a vehicle of revaluations.

As to an "anxiety of influences," this is something I've never suffered from. To the contrary, I have always felt deeply grateful to those voices that have helped me develop my own; those doors – those marvellous doors – that each of us must pass through in order to reach, at last, a room of our own.

There is always, I think, an element of discomfort in exile; what is your actual relationship with the U.S. and the literary milieu?

I can honestly say, after thirty-five years abroad, that I haven't suffered a single moment's discomfort due to exile. To the contrary, I've always considered it a privilege to live "off center," at a full remove from my own linguistic milieu, along a kind of cultural margin in which the words, far from all possible banalization, are free to take on totally unexpected weights, resonances, textures. Thanks to that very distance, what's more, the words are quick to enter into fresh alliances, entirely new combinations, fuse in any number of surprising ways. Exile, finally, can become a kind of license for a poet, a context out of context, an empty chamber in which the only music is that of one's own astonished murmurs.

As to my actual relationship with the U.S., I'd probably have been more accepted, established, "successful" in terms of grants, fellowships and the like, if I'd remained within its confines, frequented a particular literary milieu, etc., but then, would I have said the same things? Written the same works? I have the impression that everything I've managed to write has emanated out of a succession of edges: the edge, first, of consciousness, operating, in turn, at the edge – the geographic, linguistic edge – of a given culture while moving, at the same time, along the very extremities of yet another edge: that of a particular, historical order. If anything, my poetry might be considered "liminal," "peripheral" in the most literal sense of those terms. My entire work, in fact, might be seen as a transcript of sorts, celebrating margins.

My next questions would touch on the way you work. How does a poem begin: a place, a word, light?

Invariably, the poem, for me, begins with a single, sharply defined perception: with what I call a "palpable." Out of that "palpable" the poem is free to evolve if that initial image satisfies two, absolutely essential conditions: that it generate – set into play – a sequence of associated images, echoes and reflections; and secondly, that it contain, within its initiating sound-cluster, the yet unravelled sonorities of the poem-to-come. Yes, within that instigating image, both the sense and sound of the entire poem must already lie latent, imminent-like seeds in a seed-pod. For my own writing, method consists of drawing out of each, successive image – beginning with the very first – the hidden implications of those that follow. The poem, thereby, arises as if out of itself rather than out of some imposed, predetermined schema of my own. I compose, then, by accretion, by the adjustment of one syllable to the next, obeying what I feel the poem wishes to say as an autonomous force unto itself. I could never have "thought" my poem in advance, predicted its trajectory. For all my meticulous adjustments, it's the poem, finally, that speaks, not the poet. The poem, finally, that allows for disclosure.

Do you always have to write in only one place or can you be nomadic?

I've occasionally written in cafés, restaurants, hotel bedrooms, but the better part of my work has come out of a tiny, two-meter-by-three *cabanon* I built for myself a quarter of a century ago at the very edge of an almond orchard. It's there, fixed in space and held to a rigorous, even monotonous work schedule, that my work comes free. There that the movement, the pulsation of the poem can best be generated. Clearly, a direct rapport exists between my own rather monastic work habits and the release – the liberation – of all those adjusted syllables.

Why are your lines usually short and why does your strophe seem to fall rather than rest in any given place?

Here again, it's a question of movement, pulsation: a question of breaking with what I consider the linear stasis of the traditional line wherein one reads left-to-right then, at line's end, catches one's breath and begins again, a few millimeters lower, etc., etc. Why impose such a rigid structure on the elasticity of phenomena? I want the eye to fall, plummet, tumble like water over the lines – the ledges – of the poem (long lines in which the movement's suspended, short ones in which it's accelerated); yes, fall like a cascade with all the natural force of gravity itself. In this sense, I've been somewhat influenced by film, by film strip. For there, too, the cadence is determined by an inexorable movement downward, by a kind of optical plummeting. There's nothing to stop it, either, least of all some arbitrary law of prosody. The eye falls, ideally, at the very rate the given images (like so many cinematic frames) come, successively, to replace one another in each, carefully orchestrated sequence.

Why don't you use capital letters? These questions might appear innocent but I think a description of method points in reality to a poetics. Would you agree?

Yes, I entirely agree, for choices such as these – i.e., the omission of capitals, etc. – are deliberate and do, indeed, go to determine a poetic.

Regarding capitals, I've always found them somewhat divisive in verse. Within the running poem, they set up a tiny, typographical hierarchy that I've always considered slightly imperious. This, though, might be nothing more than a vestige of all that reading I did as an adolescent: all these back issues, for instance, of *the transatlantic review* (sic) that turned out to be so determinant.

The poems themselves. There are many recurrent words: mirrors, crystals, octave, blown, relic. But among them, breath seems to be the guiding vocable. Could you explain why?

First of all, breath is how we, as living creatures, transact with air, with everything, in fact, that surrounds us. Inhaling, exhaling, it's our system of exchange – our invisible currency-with the world at large. Inseparably, it's by the bias of breath that language, expelled from the body, travels towards its ever-attendant reception. Yes, every bit as much linguistic, physiological, breath – the "breath-of-life" as it's often called in Amerindian cultures – is treated as the very vector of existence itself.

The body always has a fragmented presence in your poems, it is never completely there, as if one had only the possibility of seeing parts, never the whole. And in general, your poems refer basically to wrists, ankles, hair. It is like a Duchamp painting in an impressionist landscape. Also, in a sense, it is as if everything was always being broken down by movement. Could you give me a clue?

In my poetry, I deliberately select images that depict some critical detail, some meaningful element, be it that of a body, a cloud or, say, the volutes found on either side of some baroque entablature. I proceed by successive frames: by the eloquence found, that is, in so many selected particulars. For it's these, I feel, that travel furthest. Arising out of some intimate observation, they best withstand – it would seem – the distances into which, lyrically, they're cast.

This movement, sequential by nature, is the opposite of Duchamp's analytic breakdown of composite elements. Here, one image, in tight succession, comes to reinforce the next. The parts, in turn, are offered up as integral contributions to the whole: the poem, that is, as sole totality.

Landscape is fundamental in your poetry, not because it is being described, but because it is threatened by perception. Is this true?

In discussing my work, a literary critic once called me a landscape poet whose terrain happens to be language. I can only agree, of course. Even if optically my poems seem to plummet, semantically they tend to stretch, extend laterally across a given expanse, move in the direction of their own potential reception. This landscape, however, is a perilous one. Given that it's composed of words, and words alone, the trajectory of the poem – its very *démarche* – is continuously threatened, no, not by perception (for me, perception can only save, rescue) but by misnomer. For the rocks, here, are never more than "rocks," than nominal entities. And the further one progresses in the poem, the more fragile, tenuous, susceptible they become: the more dependant, that is, the mineral grows on its given murmur, substance on its given substantive.

Where, though, do these landscapes lead? Towards what, in fact, is the poem headed? And what indeed do I mean by the poem's "potential reception?" Received where, exactly? For it struck me in reviewing my entire work three years ago for a selected edition that virtually every poem I've written is aimed, directed. Invariably, they're each trying to *get somewhere.*

There's an insistence, for example, running throughout on participles such as "drawn," "driven," "impelled;" on prepositions such as "to," "towards," "through;" on each and every verbal element, in short, that might express movement, suggest passage. Furthermore, the poem, at one crucial moment or another, often changes tense, goes from time past or time present to time conditional: from, that is, a context of memories, experiences, perceptions, to one of inferences, implications, to the scarcely perceptible rumors of some inherent promise. A certain messianic pressure seems to inform the syllables as the poem journeys from a "was" to a "would", from an event to a posited eventuality; from the "votive," as I've called it in my *ars poetica*, to the "iconic."

I've done nothing more in poetry, I feel, than track, across a semantic landscape, an intuition in the direction of the intuited; a desire, call it, in the direction of the desired. For the poem, as I see it, is profoundly motivated. Lighter than the very air it travels through, it aims, ultimately, at entering the aura of its own resonance, at hearing itself heard in the shower of its own, sonorous particles, conflating, thereby, the distance between "here" and "there;" between "wish" and "wished for."

Do you think that the ideal place is equal to the ideal language? That is, that once you have found the right word you have found the right place?

The "ideal place," I feel, is illusory (wouldn't any expatriate say the same?) and the "ideal word," inexistent. There are, however, correlatives that exist between certain places and certain words that could, at the very limit, be considered ideal in themselves. For example, in the Pueblo creation myth, it's said that the very first people were instructed to sing as they travelled across the surface of the earth in search of their founding settlements. They were told that when they came, eventually, to a place – a rock cliff – in which the echo of their voices perfectly replicated the song (call it, the poem) they were singing, they'd have reached, at last, their true home. This place, incidentally, called Haako in the creation myth (i.e. *Echo*), is located in present-day Acoma, New Mexico.

No, it's not the place, not the word that's ideal, but the according of one to the other: the creation, in short, of dyads.

Isn't this, finally, what the poem would accomplish? At the end of its journey, at the extreme edge of those "semantic landscapes," there where the "word" of the poem finally "reverberates" against the written surface of the page, wouldn't it serve, even momentarily, as our sonorous mirror? A place in which we might, even if rarely, hear and – in hearing – recognize ourselves?

You are an archaeologist. I think your poetry is fragmented under this influence. You are always breaking something away: what is behind what you see? What is the archaeology of your poetry?

My poems move, as I've already suggested, from a world of circumstance to one of ideation: from one, that is, of invocation, charged with image, to that, purely sonorous, of the subject invoked. For the poem to transit from one world to another, however, the images themselves – the "palpables," that is – need to undergo total transmutation; need to be boned, gutted of every fiber that might still withhold them within the confines of the circumstantial. For the poem, as I see it, doesn't gather, but depletes; doesn't fill, but – to the contrary – narrows, contracts, wedges its way, inexorable, towards reception. It's as if the very contents of the poem needed to be sacrificed in the name of the one entity that, in this instance, finally mattered: the poem itself, that is, as its own recipient. The images, "lessened into immensity," become in turn the hollow receptacles in which the verb, at last, might reverberate. In which the empty horn of the cornucopia might fill, no, not with fruit, but with the vaporous weight of each fruit's exact vocable. It's as if one's breath, lips, mouth, in initiating the poem, had, as their secret ambition, that of creating – as their ultimate artefact – the resonant shell of a perfectly receptive ear.

I realize that the direction I've taken throughout my entire work might be considered narrow, selective, even – perhaps – parochial. I'd like to think, however, that I've been tracking, from the very start, the vestiges of a lost and once essential rhetoric: that in which invisible entities were originally addressed. You ask, what is the archeology of my poetry? And I'd answer this, just this: the excavation of those very conduits in which murmur, whisper, entreaty once channelled. The very vectors, that is, on which the words, motivated by necessity and directed toward those hallucinatory figures, once transited. Even if language, today, no longer addresses any such figures, it can, nonetheless, serve as a reflective surface wherein the words, rather than evaporating, resound. Wherein language, at last, comes to language's recourse. And serves, **so** doing, consciousness itself.

Who is the second person in your poems? Rarely do they speak in the first person. Why?

Sometime ago, I shifted from the use of the first person pronoun to that of the second as a means of distancing the "me" from myself. The "you" has an anonymous quality that I particularly appreciate, a sense of being anyone's and belonging already to a certain elsewhere: those "semantic landscapes," perhaps, I spoke of earlier. Then, too, the "you" can refer, simultaneously, to both writer and reader. It's a word that – deliberately playing on its own ambivalence – invites the two, ever-estranged participants in any given text to a certain complicity. The "you," after all, could be you. Could be you and you again. Could, in fact, very well be you, Tedi López, and most befittingly so.

Tedi López Mills (b. 1959, Mexico City) has published twelve books of poetry. Prizes she has won include the Efraín Huerta National Literature Prize, the José Fuentes Mares National Literature Prize, and the Xavier Villaurrutia Prize, Mexican literature's most prestigious award, for her book *Muerte en la rúa Augusta* (translated as *Death on Rua Augusta* by David Shook, and published by Eyewear, London). A collection of her essays in Robin Myers' translation was published as *The Book of Explanations* by Deep Vellum, Dallas, TX, in 2022, which also issued her poetry volume, *Against the Current* (*Contracorriente*) in 2016.

She still lives in Mexico City and, apart from poetry, essays and one novel, she is well-known as a translator from English and French.

www.ingramcontent.com/pod-product-compliance
Lightning Source LLC
Chambersburg PA
CBHW032146160426
43197CB00008B/794